# EDGE BOOKS™

## BLOODIEST BATTLES

# A NATION TORN APART

## APART

### THE BATTLE OF GETTYSBURG

BY SEAN STEWART PRICE

CONSULTANT:
Tim Solie
Adjunct Professor of History
Minnesota State University, Mankato

## Capstone press®

Mankato, Minnesota

Edge Books are published by Capstone Press,
151 Good Counsel Drive, P.O. Box 669, Mankato, Minnesota 56002.
www.capstonepress.com

*Library of Congress Cataloging-in-Publication Data*
Price, Sean.
    A nation torn apart : the Battle of Gettysburg / by Sean Stewart Price.
    p. cm. — (Edge books. Bloodiest battles)
    Includes bibliographical references and index.
    Summary: "Describes events before, during, and after the
Battle of Gettysburg, including key players, weapons, and battle
tactics" — Provided by publisher.
    ISBN-13: 978-1-4296-2297-4 (hardcover)
    ISBN-10: 1-4296-2297-0 (hardcover)
    1. Gettysburg, Battle of, Gettysburg, Pa., 1863 — Juvenile literature.
I. Title. II. Series.
E475.53.P89 2009
973.7'349 — dc22                                                    2008025892

**Editorial Credits**

Aaron Sautter, editor; Bob Lentz, set designer; Kim Brown,
    book designer/illustrator; Jo Miller, photo researcher

**Photo Credits**

Alamy/The London Art Archive, 10; Mary Evans Picture Library, 4;
    North Wind Picture Archives, 20–21
DEFENSEIMAGERY.MIL, 24
Getty Images Inc./Hulton Archive, 16, 26; Hulton Archive/Mathew
    Brady, 13; Hulton Archive/Library of Congress, 29; Popperfoto/
    Bob Thomas, 22–23; Stock Montage, 27
Library of Congress, cover, 8, 9, 14–15

1 2 3 4 5 6 14 13 12 11 10 09

# TABLE OF CONTENTS

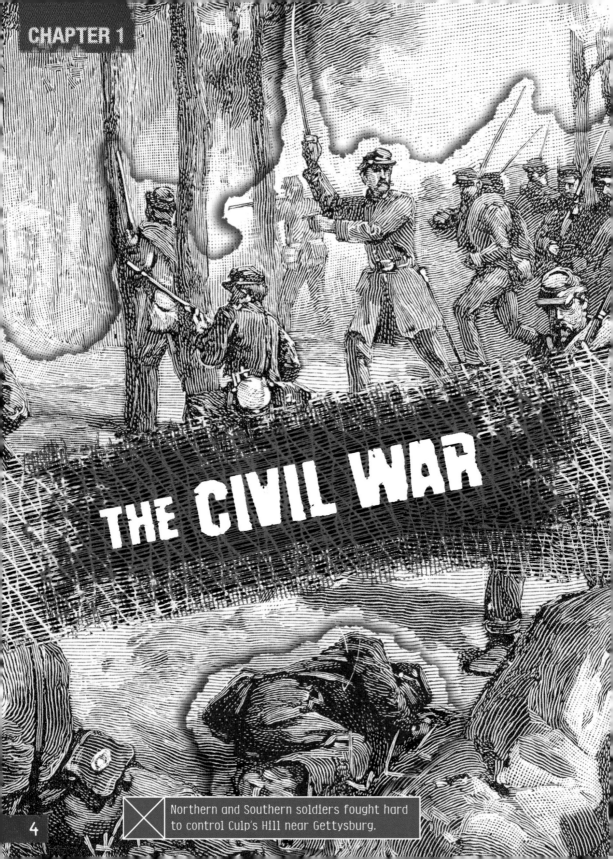

# CHAPTER 1

# THE CIVIL WAR

Northern and Southern soldiers fought hard to control Culp's Hill near Gettysburg.

On July 1, 1863, Wesley Culp marched toward his hometown of Gettysburg, Pennsylvania. The green hills were all familiar to him. Culp knew each farm and shop. His family still lived there.

But on this day, Culp was an invader. Before the Civil War (1861–1865), he had moved to Virginia to take a job. When the war broke out, he wanted to prove that he was a true Southerner. He joined the South's Confederate army. But in Pennsylvania, his family remained loyal to the North.

During the Battle of Gettysburg, Culp fought and died in the same fields where he had once worked and played. Some soldiers said he was killed near Culp's Hill, which was part of his uncle's farm. After the battle, Culp's sisters tried to find his body on the battlefield. But they found only a part of his rifle. Wesley Culp was one of about 51,000 **casualties** in the bloodiest battle in American history.

casualty — a soldier who is missing, captured, injured, or killed in battle

5

## The "Brothers War"

The Civil War was fought over two main issues. One issue was slavery. The North opposed slavery. But Southerners wanted to keep African Americans as slaves. The Southern states were also concerned about states' rights. They thought the U.S. government was becoming too powerful. They believed the U.S. Constitution gave them the right to **secede** from the Union. But President Abraham Lincoln believed the states should stay together as one country.

By the middle of 1861, 11 states had decided to leave the Union and form their own country. They called themselves the Confederate States of America, or the Confederacy. They elected Jefferson Davis of Mississippi as their president.

Before the war, families often disagreed about slavery and states' rights. When fighting broke out, family members often chose to fight for different sides. Relatives and close friends sometimes fought to the death on the battlefield. The fighting caused deep splits in many families. For this reason, the Civil War is often called the "Brothers War."

DAKOTA TERRITORY

NEBRASKA TERRITORY

MEXICO

**secede** — to formally withdraw from a group or organization

BRITISH
NORTH AMERICA

N

| 0 | 200 Mi. |
| 0 | 322 Km |

MAINE

NEW HAMPSHIRE

VERMONT

MINNESOTA

WISCONSIN

NEW YORK

MASSACHUSETTS

MICHIGAN

RHODE
ISLAND

CONNECTICUT

IOWA

PENNSYLVANIA

NEW JERSEY

# UNITED STATES OF AMERICA

GETTYSBURG

DELAWARE

MARYLAND

ILLINOIS

INDIANA

OHIO

WEST
VIRGINIA

VIRGINIA

WASHINGTON, D.C.

RICHMOND

KANSAS

MISSOURI

KENTUCKY

ATLANTIC
OCEAN

NORTH
CAROLINA

INDIAN
TERRITORY

ARKANSAS

TENNESSEE

SOUTH
CAROLINA

= UNION AND
CONFEDERATE
BOUNDARY

= FREE STATE

MISSISSIPPI

ALABAMA

GEORGIA

= SLAVE STATE

= U.S. TERRITORY

# CONFEDERATE STATES OF AMERICA

FLORIDA

= BORDER STATE
LOYAL TO USA

★ = CAPITAL CITY

TEXAS

LOUISIANA

■ = CITY

## > FIGHTING NEIGHBORS

GULF OF
MEXICO

FACT

Much of the fighting in the Civil War took place
in Virginia. Washington, D.C., and the Confederate
capital of Richmond, Virginia, were just 100 miles
(161 kilometers) apart.

## The South Moves North

By 1863, the North had scored some victories in the war. But overall, things had gone badly for the Union. Its top generals had proven ineffective or unwilling to fight.

The war was going much better for the South. General Robert E. Lee was the main commander of the Confederate army. He had led the South to several stunning victories. He defeated the Union at the Second Battle of Bull Run, the Battle of Fredericksburg, and the Battle of Chancellorsville.

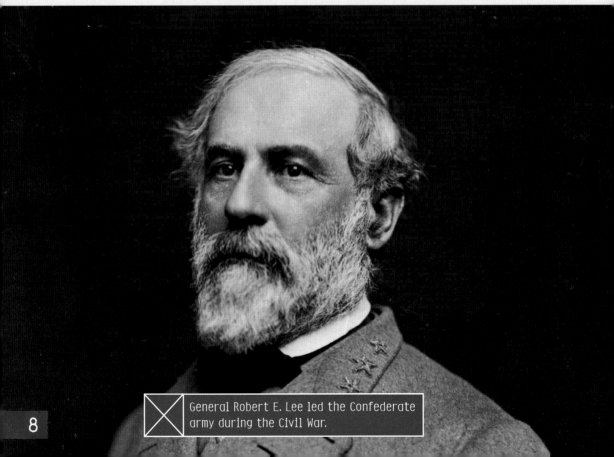

General Robert E. Lee led the Confederate army during the Civil War.

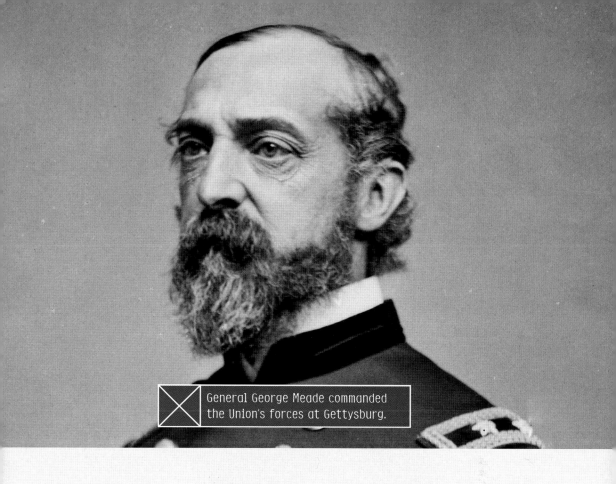

General George Meade commanded the Union's forces at Gettysburg.

In the summer of 1863, Lee decided to take the fight to northern soil. He wanted to damage the North's ability to fight. He chose to **invade** Pennsylvania. Lee thought if the South successfully invaded the North, the war would end quickly.

President Lincoln had just made General George Meade a Union commander. Meade had some success fighting the South earlier in the war. Now he was determined to stop Lee's invading army.

**invade** — to send armed forces into another country to control part of its territory

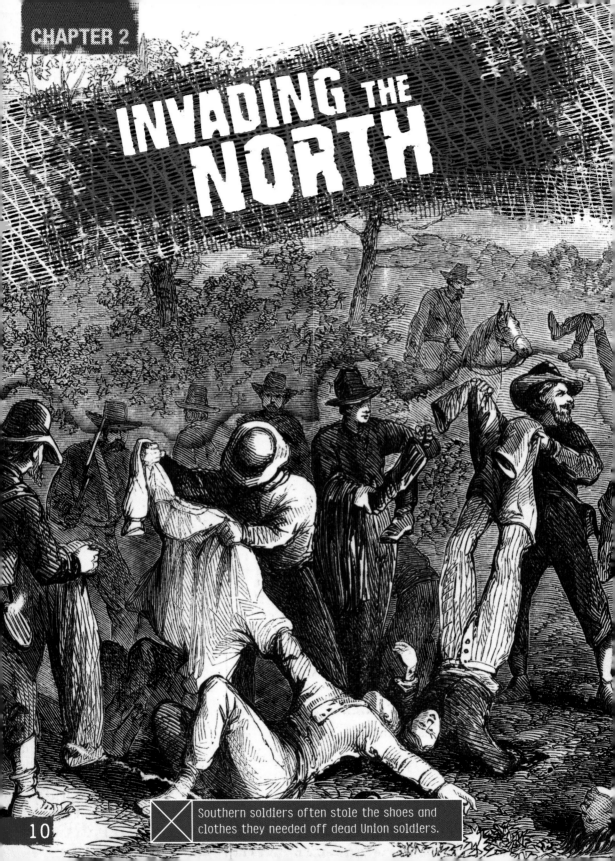

# CHAPTER 2

# INVADING THE NORTH

Southern soldiers often stole the shoes and clothes they needed off dead Union soldiers.

During the Civil War, soldiers on each side lived under very different conditions. Union soldiers usually had plenty of food and good uniforms. The North also had more men who could fight in the war. But the Southern army was poorer. Confederate soldiers had fewer supplies like shoes and blankets. They often had little food and wore worn-out clothes. The South also had a smaller population than the North. Its army had fewer soldiers to fight.

Part of the reason Lee invaded the North was for supplies. He knew Pennsylvania had food, clothes, and other things his army needed.

### > YANKEES AND REBELS

FACT:

Soldiers on both sides had nicknames during the Civil War. Northern soldiers were called Yankees, while Southern soldiers were called Rebels.

## The North's Reaction

Lee also invaded the North to take some pressure off the South. Most of the fighting had taken place there. Southern states had suffered most of the damage during the war. Lee wanted to put some pressure on the North for a change.

When Lee's army invaded, panic spread through Pennsylvania. Northerners feared the Confederates would rob or kill them. Many people buried their valuables in their gardens. Others fled their homes. Lee ordered his soldiers not to rob people, but some of them did anyway. Many Union troops had done the same thing in the South.

Meade feared Lee might attack Washington, D.C. As Lee marched north, Meade kept his army between the Southern army and the U.S. capital. That move set up an unusual situation. The Confederates actually entered Gettysburg from the north. The Union army marched in from the south.

FACT:

> THE REBEL YELL

Men on both sides used a battle cry. Union troops shouted a deep "Hurraahh!" The Confederates' "rebel yell" was more like a high-pitched scream. One soldier called it "the ugliest sound any mortal ever heard."

The Union army's powerful cannons and well-trained soldiers caused great damage in the South.

The Battle of Gettysburg was fought in the fields and hills surrounding the town.

## Why Gettysburg?

By invading the North, Lee hoped to pressure the Union into ending the war quickly. He planned to threaten Northern cities like Philadelphia and Baltimore. Lee hadn't planned on fighting in Gettysburg.

Meade didn't want to fight at Gettysburg either. He had planned to take on Lee's army about 10 miles (16 kilometers) south at Taneytown, Maryland. He thought it would draw the Confederate army out of Pennsylvania and away from the North.

Why did the two armies meet at Gettysburg? Gettysburg was a crossroad town. At least 10 major roads crossed there. Both armies were marching to different locations when they happened to meet at Gettysburg by accident.

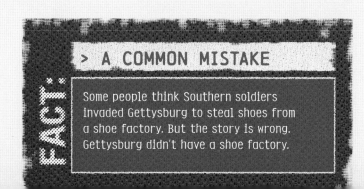

FACT:

> A COMMON MISTAKE

Some people think Southern soldiers invaded Gettysburg to steal shoes from a shoe factory. But the story is wrong. Gettysburg didn't have a shoe factory.

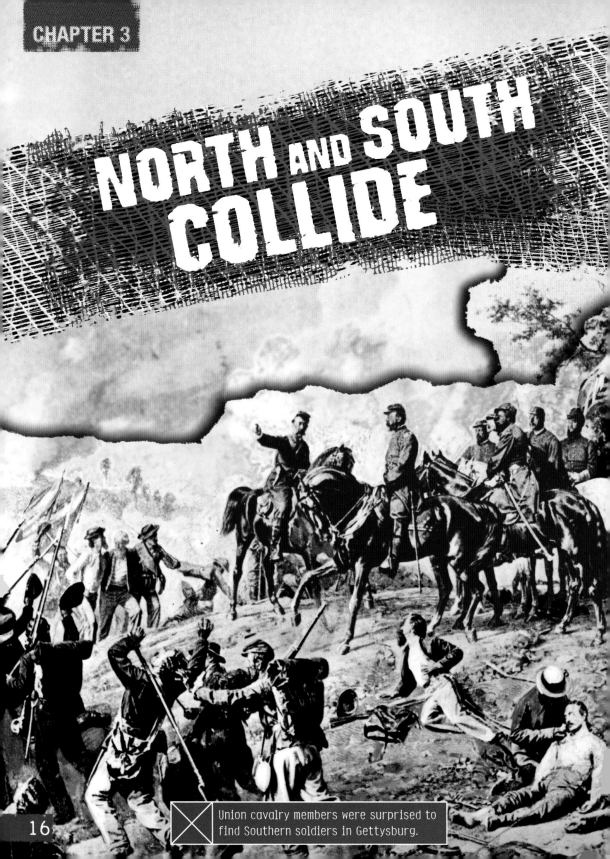

# CHAPTER 3

# NORTH AND SOUTH COLLIDE

Union cavalry members were surprised to find Southern soldiers in Gettysburg.

The Battle of Gettysburg began at 5:30 in the morning on July 1, 1863. Union **cavalry** members spotted a small group of Southern soldiers just west of Gettysburg. The Union soldiers sent for help. Then they opened fire.

The steady crackling of rifle fire filled the air. Booming cannons rattled windowpanes. Gettysburg's residents soon found their homes, churches, and shops turned into hospitals. Injured and dying men were crowded side by side. Many groaned or cried out in pain.

The Union troops were outnumbered on the first day of battle. By 4:00 in the afternoon, they had to fall back. Their faces were black with gunpowder and dirt. Their wool uniforms were soaked with sweat. They headed south through town, looking stunned and hopeless. The South had won the first day of fighting. But the battle wasn't over yet. Just south of town, more Union troops were arriving.

**cavalry** — soldiers who travel and fight on horseback

## The Fighting Continues

After the first day, both Meade and Lee rushed more troops to Gettysburg. Men marched all night to get there in time. The following day, they were thrown into the fight.

The Union troops made their stand on the hills and ridges near the town. Their lines stretched from Culp's Hill in the north to Big Round Top in the south.

The Confederates attacked up and down the Union lines all day. Many soldiers fought and died in the nearby peach orchards and wheat fields. They also fought in a rocky area called the Devil's Den. Men hit with **minié balls** often spun around and died where they stood. The wounded screamed in pain for help. But their cries were drowned out by huge explosions and the shouts of battle.

**minié ball** — a cone-shaped bullet with a hollow base that expanded outward when fired

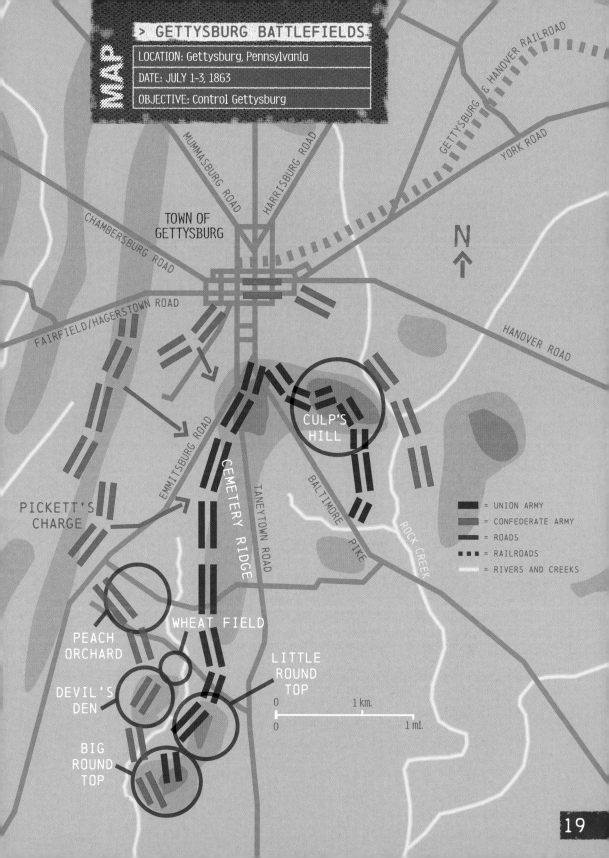

## > GETTYSBURG BATTLEFIELDS

**LOCATION:** Gettysburg, Pennsylvania

**DATE:** JULY 1–3, 1863

**OBJECTIVE:** Control Gettysburg

GETTYSBURG & HANOVER RAILROAD

MUMMASBURG ROAD

HARRISBURG ROAD

YORK ROAD

CHAMBERSBURG ROAD

TOWN OF GETTYSBURG

N

FAIRFIELD/HAGERSTOWN ROAD

HANOVER ROAD

EMMITSBURG ROAD

CULP'S HILL

PICKETT'S CHARGE

CEMETERY RIDGE

TANEYTOWN ROAD

BALTIMORE PIKE

ROCK CREEK

■ = UNION ARMY

■ = CONFEDERATE ARMY

▬ = ROADS

▪▪▪ = RAILROADS

= RIVERS AND CREEKS

WHEAT FIELD

PEACH ORCHARD

LITTLE ROUND TOP

DEVIL'S DEN

0        1 km.

0        1 mi.

BIG ROUND TOP

## Little Round Top

Some of the heaviest fighting on the second day of battle took place at Little Round Top. The South wanted to take this high ground from the Union troops. They could then fire their cannons into the Union army below.

The Confederates charged up Little Round Top many times. Each time, they almost took the hill. But the Union soldiers forced them back. After two hours, one-third of the Union men were either dead or wounded. Those left standing were almost out of ammunition.

The Confederates tried to take control of Little Round Top several times on the second day of battle.

Finally, Union commander Colonel Joshua Chamberlain risked a desperate gamble. In spite of his men's weakened condition, he ordered them to charge the Confederates. The attack worked. The Southern soldiers were exhausted from marching all night and fighting all day. The Union attack shocked them into either giving up or running away.

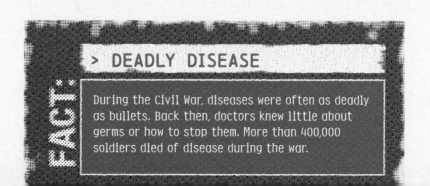

FACT:

> DEADLY DISEASE

During the Civil War, diseases were often as deadly as bullets. Back then, doctors knew little about germs or how to stop them. More than 400,000 soldiers died of disease during the war.

## Pickett's Charge

On the third day of battle, Lee ordered an all-out attack.
He chose General George Pickett to lead the main charge. That
afternoon, more than 12,000 Confederate soldiers marched
toward the Union lines. They walked in tight formations over
open ground for almost 1 mile (1.6 kilometers).

Pickett's Charge was doomed to fail. The Union
army's position was too strong.

Though impressive, the South's attack never stood a chance. First, Union cannons killed dozens of Confederates at a time. Then Union soldiers started shooting from behind a stone wall. Thousands of Southern soldiers crumpled under the heavy gunfire.

Still, Pickett's men marched bravely through a hail of bullets and cannon fire. Their attack broke the Union line briefly in one place. But Union soldiers soon pushed them back. More than half of Pickett's men were killed, wounded, or captured. The Battle of Gettysburg was finally over.

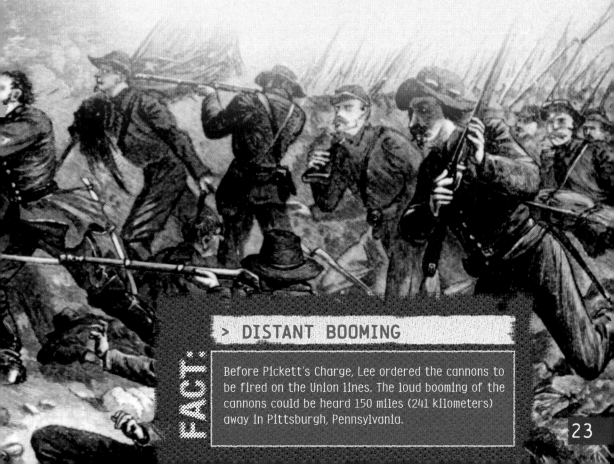

FACT:

> DISTANT BOOMING

Before Pickett's Charge, Lee ordered the cannons to be fired on the Union lines. The loud booming of the cannons could be heard 150 miles (241 kilometers) away in Pittsburgh, Pennsylvania.

# CHAPTER 4

# THE TIDE TURNS

After the battle, thousands of dead soldiers littered the fields around Gettysburg.

The Union's victory at Gettysburg came at a high cost. During the three-day battle, 85,000 Union soldiers fought against 75,000 Confederates. The Union suffered more than 23,000 casualties. But the Confederates' defeat was even more costly. The South had nearly 28,000 casualties. With more than 51,000 casualties, the Battle of Gettysburg was the bloodiest battle in U.S. history.

News of the Union's victory reached Washington, D.C., on July 4. Huge celebrations soon broke out. The Union then received even more good news. Union General Ulysses S. Grant had captured the important city of Vicksburg, Mississippi. The defeats at Gettysburg and Vicksburg spread gloom across the South.

> DEADLY DAYS

FACT:
Gettysburg was the bloodiest multi-day battle in American history. But the bloodiest single-day battle occurred about 10 months earlier. On September 17, 1862, nearly 23,000 men were killed or wounded in one day at the Battle of Antietam.

Richmond, Virginia, was one of several cities destroyed by the Union army.

## The Southern High Tide

The Battle of Gettysburg is often called the "Southern high tide." It was a turning point in the war. The battle greatly weakened the Confederate army. The South would never again have as good a chance of winning the war.

Soon after Gettysburg, Lincoln asked Grant to take control of the Union army. Unlike previous commanders, Grant fought hard and well. He refused to quit.

Union General William Sherman also caused many problems for the South. In 1864, Sherman began his famous "March to the Sea." Sherman's men destroyed most of the railroads, homes, farms, and factories from Atlanta, Georgia, to the Atlantic Ocean. Faced with homelessness and starvation, the South's desire to fight soon faded.

The combination of Grant's and Sherman's victories overwhelmed the South. Finally, Lee surrendered his army on April 9, 1865. Soon the rest of the South gave up as well. The Civil War was over.

General Lee (seated at left) surrendered his army to General Grant (seated at right) at Appomattox Court House, Virginia.

## A New Hope for Freedom

On November 19, 1863, Lincoln visited the battlefield at Gettysburg. He went to help dedicate a cemetery for the Union troops killed there. The featured speaker that day talked about the battle for two hours. Lincoln spoke for only about two minutes. Yet his speech is still remembered to this day. Lincoln's Gettysburg Address is one of the most quoted speeches in U.S. history.

In his speech, Lincoln promised that the dead soldiers at Gettysburg didn't die without a reason. He promised that they would be remembered for their sacrifice. He also promised that the freedoms given by the U.S. government would never end.

The Battle of Gettysburg was a turning point in the Civil War. The North's victory gave new life to the Union's war effort. When the war was over, slavery finally ended. The states remained together as one nation. Today visitors can see hundreds of monuments honoring the dead at Soldiers' National Cemetery and the Gettysburg National Military Park.

President Lincoln's Gettysburg Address is considered one of the greatest speeches in U.S. history.

# GLOSSARY

**ammunition** (am-yuh-NI-shuhn) — bullets and other objects that can be fired from weapons

**casualty** (KAZH-oo-uhl-tee) — a soldier who is missing, captured, injured, or killed in battle

**cavalry** (KA-vuhl-ree) — soldiers who travel and fight on horseback

**invade** (in-VADE) — to send armed forces into another country to control part of its territory

**minié ball** (min-ee-AY BAWL ) — a cone-shaped bullet with a hollow base that expanded outward when fired

**secede** (si-SEED) — to formally withdraw from a group or an organization, often to form another organization

**slavery** (SLAY-vur-ee) — the owning of other people; slaves are forced to work without pay.

**surrender** (suh-REN-dur) — to give up or admit defeat

# READ MORE

**Burgan, Michael.** *The Battle of Gettysburg.* Graphic History. Mankato, Minn.: Capstone Press, 2006.

**Fradin, Dennis B.** *The Battle of Gettysburg.* Turning Points in U.S. History. New York: Marshall Cavendish Benchmark, 2008.

**Hale, Sarah Elder, ed.** *Gettysburg: Bold Battle in the North.* The Civil War. Peterborough, N.H.: Cobblestone, 2005.

# INTERNET SITES

FactHound offers a safe, fun way to find educator-approved Internet sites related to this book.

Here's what to do:
1. Visit www.facthound.com
2. Choose your grade level.
3. Begin your seach.

This book's ID number is 9781429622974.

FactHound will fetch the best sites for you!

# INDEX